# Jokes & Gags

## For the stage show entertainer.

## Another collection of humor, satire, gags, jokes, and bits of business

*Whether you are Comedy team, standup comic, ventriloquist or just a person who likes telling jokes You will find some great material here.*

## L. Wade Johnson

This is book 2. I would have put all these jokes into book 1 but I did not discover them until I had

already published book 1. SO, I also, I dedicate this book to me for without me I would not have discovered jokes I thought I had lost and therefore this book would have never been written.

This is no ordinary joke book, it was written for the performer who wants laughs. If its Laughs you want you got them here, sure fire tested, wholesome comedy material.

Included in this material are set up lines, comedy activities, one liners and general funny stuff organized by topic for the stage show entertainer.

A comedian is a person who comes on stage in front of millions of people with problems and makes them laugh.

Printed in Inglesh

ISBN-172032171X

ISBN-9781720321712

*You know, sometimes I sit quietly and wonder why I'm not in an insane asylum. Then I take a look around and think, maybe I already am.*

## Acknowledgements

Over the past 62 years I have worked with many funny people. Those who provided encouragement, like my dad, James R. Johnson Sr. and my Grandfather C. J. Johnson both of whom were talented stage show personalities doing magic using comedy material.

Included in the list of those of whom I have benefited are Don Campbell, the leader of the band that went with me to many contests and stage shows and my television show. James D. Purple who paved the way for me to get my first real break. John Phillips Sr. and John Phillips Jr.

To my wife, Sharon Amore Thomas Johnson who put up with my jokes and overall silliness for the past fifty plus years. There must be a special place in God's kingdom for wives like her. She passed away on January 12, 2018 so my laughter has diminished somewhat since then.

## Contents

## Age and aging

My birthday candles cost more than the cake.

When I was child I thought a nap was punishment. Now its like a mini vacation.

My people skills are alright, it's those idiots I work with that needs work

Oh, I don't have to write it down I can remember it.

Getting lucky means I walk into a room and remember what I went in there for.

To me, happy hour is a nap,

## Air Conditioning

This place is air conditioned.  Have you ever seen air in such a condition?

We have an unusual breakdown with the air conditioning system. The delivery truck broke down three years ago.

It's cold in here. I think management likes the thermostat set to Siberia.

Hey colder than a well diggers butt in this place.

## Armed Forces

What a sergeant! His voice has stripes in it.

Sergeant: Doesn't these stripes mean anything to you?
Soldier: Hey, a zebra is covered with them and underneath he is still a jackass.
I got a G.I. haircut when I got to boot camp. That was several years ago, and it hasn't healed yet.

## Automobiles and driving

A little old lady was driving a big car through a construction zone when she ran over a man. She opened her car door and shouted, "Young man you better watch out!" To that the man shouted back; "my gosh lady don't tell me you're gonna back up!"

According to the National Safety Council there will be over 420 deaths due to automobile accidents this holiday season. So far, only 300 have been killed. Some of you folks aren't trying.

I just put a new gadget in my car that keeps it quiet inside. It fits over her mouth.

Now, that was a powerful car. It can climb any hill without a strain. The problem is, it got too confident it tried to climb a lamp post.

Now, just think about this. Henry Ford. He must have been a humble man. In spite of all his riches, he never owned a Cadillac.

Now days when you drive 55 you are double parked.

Talk about bad luck! I bought a set so snow tires and the melted.

He says it is an antique car. That means a Cadillac that is no longer under warranty.

If all cars in the United States were lined up end to end it would be Labor Day weekend.

I can tell you, since I bought that car there has been one happy man in town. The salesman.

That is the only car in town held together by a paint job.

Someone stole my car last night when I was in the restaurant. I was going to report it to the police, but then I remembered my mother-in-law was asleep in the back seat. I figure when she wakes up the thief will return it.

Well, yes, it is, a nice car. I cost me 12 installments and a change of address.

We like to drive down the road and watch the pedestrians whiz by.

It is an old car.  To give you some idea how old, it takes upper and lower license plates.

What's this? A parking ticket? You should give me a medal.

She drives a vehicle that four hundred dollars to the mile. She calls it a shopping cart.

He calls it an antique, but it is just old. It needs upper and lower license plates.

I wish my car was a year older. Then it would be paid for.

I am giving up driving in the city. I just don't have the vocabulary for it.

## Baldy Jokes

He's mad tonight. He spent twenty minutes combing his hair and then forgot to bring it with him.

Did you get caught in the wind and the rain? I did. It is a bad hair day. I couldn't do a thing with my hair. So, I left it home.

He combs his hair with a sponge.

I have seen more hair on a piece of bacon.

Yes, I'm bald. But you got to admit it's neat.

Ah huh, I see you got in an argument with your barber again.

Well, yes but when unexpected company drops in all I have to do is straighten my tie.

You left your head wide open for that one.

He got a crew cut. It looks like the crew bailed out.

## Bands, Orchestra, Musicians.

Are you're the conductor? I want a transfer.

Get a load of the band. Looks like a police lineup on a Monday morning.

Is that a new drummer, or did the old one take a bath?

They have never played better. Kinda sad when you think about it.

He plays the hottest guitar in town. He stole it two hours ago.

An Accordion player is the only musician who can play both ends against the middle.

Ladies and gentlemen let's have a round of applause for our piano player. The Steinway piano company has asked me to tell you this is a Baldwin piano.

This is (name) our tuba player. Now there is a guy who is wrapped up in his work.

He plays by ear too bad he's hard of hearing.

(Lift cymbal) What! Pot roast again?

In case you are wandering what, the paper is in front of the conductor, it is the score. I think the drummer is winning.

You call that music? Sounds like a beer truck running over a warped manhole cover.

He also plays the steel guitar, not that I can how he got it.

Band leader (or conductor) looks at you. Don't look at me, turn around and face the music.

He also plays the steel guitar, although I don't care how he got it.

(Band playing too loud) Ah fellas could you hold it down a little, I can still hear you.

(Band leader faces you) Hey, don't look at me, turn around and face the music.


## Beauty Contest

They held a beauty contest in that town last month. Nobody won.

She entered the Miss America contest and darn near lost her citizenship.


## Bits of Business for the entertainer
Plug these into your routine

The combination to the lock is the same as my wife's birthday. 6-23-44. No, wait, that is her measurements.

Teacher finds picture of a nude lady in his text book. He demands an explanation. "Is that your picture?" he asks. The student replies; "I don't think so, it doesn't look like me."

Dying scene. Stumble around until someone puts a bucket in front of you. Kick it and then, lie down.
Scantily clothed girl. I can tell just by looking at you that you aren't hiding anything.

He is an usher. Now there is a guy who really puts people in their place.
Black eye. Nasty battle with a grapefruit.

Beautiful girl with sexy gate. "Oh, if only my watch had a movement like that."

Don't laugh. Lady, your daughter may be in here.

Don't look now, but there is one too many people in this room and I think it's you.


Ventriloquist dummy disappears. Dummy pops up in the chest of drawers, cabinet, closet, box on the table (other places).

Spooky scene:
I don't want to see a real live skeleton.
Have you ever seen a real live skeleton?
No, and if I do it will be too soon.

Hey, are you trying to scare somebody?
Yeah.
That's what I thought.

Dummy gets carried away with the routine (song or scene)
Ventriloquist pulls dummy back.
Oh. Excuse me folks I was beginning to enjoy myself for a while there.

Magician production number: Pull out silks, then a lot of laundry items.

Magician: (Take a cracker in left hand. Pretend slight of hand placing cracker in right hand).
"Now I just sprinkle a little magic dust over it."
(Crumble cracker let crumbs fall on left hand. Turn left hand over show empty, show right hand empty).

Magician with deck of cards. "Pick a card, any card." Hand a card to the stooge.
(Stooge is what magicians call someone from audience who agrees to work with them on a trick).

Magician has one card. O K here in my hand I have a card. I will shuffle it.

Just add a little to your laundry and it will smell as clean as all outdoors.
Out doors? This guy never lived in my neighborhood.

Lights go out. "What are they doing, closing up the joint?"

Comes out with crutches. Throw crutches away. Falls down.

If you are the undertaker, you are a day early.

I wasn't eves dropping you understand. But I couldn't help but over hear you since I was listening at the door.

Joke flops. Thank goodness next week is Dubuque.
Joke flops. That's funny. It worked in rehearsal either.

Dummy to Ventriloquist: We are going to have to make some money or learn a trade.

He is a man of convictions and they are both for drunken driving.

It will be hard to fill his shoes. It will take several shovels full.

Sit down at bar order a coke. (Turn to audience) this was a bar scene, but our producer censored it.

Magician showing a red silk. This is a green silk, died green.

Someone enters: Oh, look whose here arsenic and old face.

On telephone. "Hello, is the city bridge department? Well, how much is a 3 no trump?"

Obviously, I am dealing with an inferior mentality.

We know our product lasts 20 years. We have been in business 20 years and no one has ever come back for another one.

## Business

The fourth-grade teacher addressed her class on the first day of the school year. "I have a twenty-dollar bill, here and I will give it to the first person who can tell me the name of the most important person in history, responsible for the founding of a nation." The children guessed one name after another, none of the names were accepted by the teacher. A little Jewish boy was sitting in the back row, happened to notice an unfinished bulletin board behind her. He could see the numbers; 1492. "I think I know where she is going with this." He thought. He raised his hand and said Christopher Columbus." "You are correct, come on up here and take this twenty-dollar bill. The book took the money and sat back down. "This young man correctly identified Christopher Columbus." She said. "Actually, I was thinking of Moses, but business is business."

"I want to see you."
Make a date with my secretary."
I did but I still want to see you.

My uncle Ralph went into business for himself. He must be doing pretty well, too. I don't know what he is worth today, but last month the government was offering $1000 for him.

Fat executive: Be nice to him he has a lot of pull. He needs it with all that drag.

The Senator stands on his record. Good thing too, if he got off someone might read it.

The only one who starts at the top is a hole digger.

Better call the Better Business Bureau and tell them to send one over.

He suffers from chronic unemployment.

This is a non-profit organization, but we didn't plan it that way.

## Christmas

I have a little surprise for Santa Clause, myself, this Christmas. I lined my chimney with fish hooks

October runs into November, November runs into December, December runs into Christmas and Christmas runs into money.

Deck the halls with poison ivy.

It is nearing Christmas, I think, let's see, Septober, Octember, Nowonder.

## Church Bulletins

These sentences (read carefully) actually appeared in church bulletins or were announced at church services.

The Fasting & Prayer Conference includes meals.

Scouts are saving aluminum cans, bottles and other items to be recycled Proceeds will be used to cripple children.

The sermon this morning: 'Jesus Walks on the Water. ' The sermon tonight: 'Searching for Jesus.'

Ladies, don't forget the rummage sale. It's a chance to get rid of those things not worth keeping around the house. Bring your husbands.

Don't let worry kill you off - let the Church help

Miss Charlene Mason sang 'I will not pass this way again,' giving obvious pleasure to the congregation.

For those of you who have children and don't know it, we have a nursery downstairs.

Next Thursday there will be try-outs for the choir. They need all the help they can get.

Irving Benson and Jessie Carter were married on October 24 in the church. So ends a friendship that began in their school days.

A bean supper will be held on Tuesday evening in the church hall. Music will follow.

At the evening service tonight, the sermon topic will be 'What Is Hell?' Come early and listen to our choir practice.

Eight new choir robes are currently needed due to the addition of several new members and to the deterioration of some older ones.

Please place your donation in the envelope along with the deceased person you want remembered.

The church will host an evening of fine dining, super entertainment and gracious hostility.

Pot-luck supper Sunday at 5:00 PM - prayer and medication to follow.

The ladies of the Church have cast off clothing of every kind. They may be seen in the basement on Friday afternoon.

This evening at 7 PM there will be a hymn singing in the park across from the Church. Bring a blanket and come prepared to sin.

The pastor would appreciate it if the ladies of the Congregation would lend him their electric girdles for the pancake breakfast next
Sunday.

Low Self Esteem Support Group will meet Thursday at 7 PM. Please use the back door.

The eighth-graders will be presenting Shakespeare's Hamlet in the Church basement Friday at 7 PM. The congregation is invited to attend this tragedy.


Weight Watchers will meet at 7 PM at the First Presbyterian Church. Please use large double door at the side entrance.

The Associate Minister unveiled the church's new campaign slogan last Sunday: 'I Upped My Pledge-—Up Yours.'

Three boys were bragging about the success of their dads. "My dad puts a few notes on a paper they call it a song and he $50 for it."

The next boy says, "That's no0thing, my dad writes something on a piece of paper they call it a book and he gets $100 for it.

The third boy said; "My dad scribbles a few notes on a piece of paper, they call it a sermon and it takes eight people to collect all the money.


## Closings for the stage show entertainer

I want to thank you from the bottom of my paycheck.

Ventriloquist: You are a good audience and I want to thank you from the bottom my heart.
Dummy: I also want to thank you from my bottom.

Before I go, I would like you to give me a little help on something. When I count to three would everyone here stomp on the floor three times? (Audience stomps). Thank you. I got into an argument with the building custodian and I just wanted to irritate him.

Thank you have been a great audience. On behalf of the management, I would like to say I would like to be half of the management.

We have a great show next week. So, it you want to see what happens tune in next Tuesday.

## The Court System

I don't have too much faith in jury trials. How can you send six men and six women in a room overnight and come out and say, 'not guilty?'

Judge: When were you born?
Man: I don't know judge I was just a little baby at the time.

Judge: Guilty or not guilty"
Defendant: If I tell you now it will spoil the trial.

How do you like that? The defendant is out on bail and they locked up the jury.

Judge: Have you ever been up before me?
Defendant: I don't know judge.  What time do you get up?

Honest judge, I was smoking in bed. It was already on fire when I got into it.

Defendant: Honest judge, I wasn't drunk.
Judge: The officer that arrested you said you were climbing a lamp post.
Defendant: I had to judge, a couple of alligators were chasing me.

Judge:  The officer said you ignored that red light.
Defendant: Oh, come on judge, when you see one you have seen the all.

Defendant: O K, I'll give it to you short and fast.
Judge: An I want the truth.
Defendant: Well. . . that may take a little longer.

Judge: I can't let you go, you broke the law.
Female defendant: Well. . . can't you get a new one?

Judge: What do you mean you didn't lay a hand on her. She has a broken jaw, a bloody nose and a black eye.
Defendant: Hey, who are you going to believe, me or that punch drunk broad?

## Crooks and bad guys

There has been a robbery.
I caught one of them
Which one?
The one that was robbed.

The crooks stole my car and got away. But I got the license number.

Crime is up 15%. I think I should have invested in crime.

He stole a TV from the store in broad daylight. He would have gotten away with it except he mailed in the 90-day warranty.

He is so crooked he pays bribes in counterfeit money.

He counts his money in front of a mirror. He doesn't even trust himself.

Hey, look if you can't control crime, why not legalize it and tax it out of business?

I don't like the word stealing. I call it redistribution.

Ventriloquist: Well, you will think of something. Just use that slinky, conniving, devious mind of yours.
Dummy: You left out sneaky.

He is so crooked he has to screw on his socks

If a burglar breaks into my house all he will get is practice.

Hey, I grew up in a tough neighborhood. When we played hop scotch, we used real scotch. When we played cops and robbers we use real cops. When the Salvation Army passed the hat they didn't get it back.

He carved a pistol out of a block of wood and held up a toy store.

## **Doubles** (insert into any sketch)

You broke the law.
I did what?
You broke the law
Can't they get another one?

Did you take a bath today?
Why is one missing?

One: Where have you been, we have been waiting with open arms
Two: How late do you stay open?

One: She wanted one of my pictures.
Two: Which one did you give her?
One: The one of . . . (famous attractive movie star)

One: Call me a cab.
Two: You're a cab.

My husband is bead.
Are you sure he's not just using that for an excuse?

My husband is dead.
Your husband is not dead lady, he's hiding.

One: Where am I? Where am I?
Two: Where are you? Why you're fight here.

(Ventriloquist makes a mistake)
You'll be alright, all you need is a ventriloquist.

We had the audience glued to their seats.
Yeah, that was a sneaky way of keeping them there.

Wait, you say I am your second most favorite entertainer? Who is your most favorite.
(Name a popular animal act)

Hold your tongue.
I should hold my tongue?
You should hold your tongue.
For how long?
Till you choke.

One: What are you doing?
Two: Nothing.
One: Well, how will you know when you are finished.

One: Okay, keep your eyes open.
Two: Why?
One: Because you will look pretty stupid walking around with them closed.

One: How do you feel?
Two: Like a dog, call the veterinarian.

One: I had a tough life growing up, I tell ya it was tough.
Two: How so?
One: When I was ten my father took me swimming in the lake.
Two: Why was that so tough?
One: Everyone else were ice skating.

One: I came to get the lawn mower I lent you.
Two: Sorry, ole man I lent it to a friend of mine. Do you need it back now?
One: Not for myself no, but the fella I borrowed it from says the guy he borrowed it from needs to return it to the guy who lent it to him.

One: If you expect to do all that you will need to pay me more money.
Two: How much am I paying you now?
One: Ten dollars a week.
Two: I tell you what, from now on I will pay you thirty dollars a month.
One: Okay.

One: What makes you so stupid?
Two: I don't know but whatever it is it works.

One: What you taking for that cold?
Two: Make me an offer.

Dummy: Hey, I get the laughs around here.
Other: The only laugh you got was a sneer from disgruntled termite.

Person: I have an empty space in my life for you little pal.
Dummy: In your heart?
Person: No, in my fireplace.

The river Styx is mythological
Is that near the mithithippi?

One: Uncle Bill was a circus star. He swallowed a five-foot sword.
Two: What is so great about that, lots of sword swallowers use a five-foot sword.
One: Uncle Bill was only four foot tall. Then one day he decided to retire.
Two: retire?
One: Yeah, he got the hiccups.

One: Uncle Charlie was the guy they shot out of a cannon.
Two: That sounds dangerous, did he ever get hurt?
One: We don't know, we ain't found him yet.
Ventriloquist drops dummy's voice to a lower octave

Dummy: Hey, give me back the voice I stated with.

Vent: Please, you're interrupting me. I can't finish the song.
Dummy: You don't have to say please I'm glad to do it.

Dummy: Say, you were pretty good at that.
Vent: Well, you know how it is. Some have it and some don't.
Dummy: And you are full of it.

Ventriloquist: You're hopeless

Dummy: I'm Democrat. . . . well. . . same thing (may use Republican)

One: What time does your show go on?
Two: When can you be there?

One: So, you say you're smart?
Two: Yeah. You can ask me two questions for $20.
One: That's a high price to pay, isn't it?
Two: Yes. What is your next question?

One: I think I am losing my memory.
Two: Oh, forget about it.
One: I tell you I think I am losing my memory.
Two: How long has this been going on?
One: How long has what been going on?

Dummy: Don't laugh (vent's name) you know I can't talk when you are laughing.

I remember the first time I saw her, I just sat right down and cried.
Bawled like a baby huh?
She certainly was.

One: how, would you like a fat lip?
Two: You got one?
One: No, I do not have one.
Two: Would you like one?
One: No, I don't want one.

Vent: You know, there is a morale to this story.
Dummy: Yeah, a fool and his stories are soon started.

Please you are interrupting my act.
You don't have to say please I'm glad to do it.

We just made a record.
Yeah, we spent 132 hours in the back seat of a Volkswagen.
A new world's record.

Our last show received mixed notices
We liked it the audience didn't.

Our act has a happy ending.
You will be happy when it's over.

## Doctors, nurses, hospitals, sickness etc.

Insurance is no good. I know a guy who had a million dollars of insurance and he died anyway.
He told the doctor he only drinks to relieve his suffering. He suffers from chronic thirst for booze.

What do you mean my eyes are weak? On a clear day I can see all the way to my glasses.

I am so full of medicine every time I sneeze I cure somebody.

Sometimes I think I am losing my short-term memory. And now I think my short-term memory is going as well.
He reads the obituary column to cheer himself up.

Insanity is hereditary. You can get it from your children.

What kind of doctor are you? All your patients are sick.

My doctor told me to go to Arizona for my lungs. I don't know why he sent them there.

You have heard an apple a day keeps the doctor away. For this guy a duck a day keeps him away he's a quack.

My bookie had a disease and he went to a doctor. The doctor was a quack. He saved my bookie's life.
Obstetrician is a stork with a large bill.

If you get hurt on the job can you call that labor pains?

He went to the doctor to get a cure for kleptomania.
What's he taken for it?
Everything.

He was in the hospital for the flu. After four days he took a turn for the nurse.

Nurse looking a watch while taking pulse. What is it? Huh, oh two O'clock.

Doctor: We could do this under a local anesthetic.
Patient: Hey local or imported I don't care.

The best get-well cards are four aces.

One: The doctor is here.
Two: Tell him I can't see him. I'm sick

Nurse: O, doctor.
Doctor: Did you call me, nurse?
Nurse: No, I called you doctor.

One: My stomach hurts.
Two: Where?
One: Between my eyes and my knees

Patient: Doc it hurts when I do his
Doc: Don't do that.

Insurance is not so great. I know a guy who had hundred thousand dollars of insurance, but he died anyway.

She doesn't need an eye doctor, she needs a witch doctor.

It looks like the hospital agreed with you.
Yeah, and so did the nurses.

I am so full of medication, every time I cough I cure somebody.

Doc, I think I am losing my memory.
How long has this been going on?
How long has what been going on.

An old physician, Doctor Gordon Geezer, became very bored in retirement and decided to re-open a medical clinic. He put a sign up outside that said: "Dr. Geezer's clinic. Get your treatment for $500 - if not cured, get back $1,000."

Doctor Digger Young, who was positive that this old geezer didn't know beans about medicine, thought this would be a great opportunity to get $1,000. So, he went to Dr. Geezer's clinic.

Dr. Young: "Dr. Geezer, I have lost all taste in my mouth. Can you please help me?"

Dr. Geezer: "Nurse, please bring medicine from box 22 and put 3 drops in Dr. Young's mouth."

Dr. Young: 'Aaagh! -- This is Gasoline!"

Dr. Geezer: "Congratulations! You've got your taste back. That will be $500."

Dr. Young gets annoyed and goes back after a couple of days figuring to recover his money.

Dr. Young: "I have lost my memory, I cannot remember anything."

Dr. Geezer: "Nurse, please bring medicine from box 22 and put 3 drops in the patient's mouth."

Dr. Young: "Oh, no you don't -- that is Gasoline!"

Dr. Geezer: "Congratulations! You've got your memory back. That will be $500."

Dr. Young (after having lost $1000) leaves angrily and comes back after several more days.

Dr. Young: "My eyesight has become weak --- I can hardly see anything!"

Dr. Geezer: "Well, I don't have any medicine for that so, "Here's your $1000 back" (giving him a $10 bill).

Dr. Young: "But this is only $10!"

Dr. Geezer: "Congratulations! You got your vision back! That will be $500."

Moral of story --Just because you're "young" doesn't mean that you can outsmart an "old Geezer"

Remember: Don't make old people mad. We don't like being old in the first place, so it doesn't take much to piss us off.


## Redneck definition of Medical Terms

Artery: The study of paintings.

Bacteria: Back door to the cafeteria

Barium: What doctors do when patients die.

Benign: What you be, after you be eight.

Caesarean Section: A neighborhood in Rome.

Cauterize: Make eye contact with her.

Coma: A punctuation mark

Dilate: To live long.

Enema: Not a friend

Fester: Quicker than someone else.

Fibula: A small lie.

Labor Pain: Getting hurt at work.

Medical Staff: A doctor's cane.

Morbid: A higher offer.

Outpatient: a person who has fainted.

Post-operative: A letter carrier.

Recovery room: Place to do upholstery.

Recovery room: Where you go to use to the idea of paying the bill is forever.

Rectum: Nearly killed him     .

Secretion: Hiding something.

Seizure: A Roman Emperor.

Tablet: A small table.

Terminal illness: Getting sick at the airport.

Tumor: One plus one more

Urine: Opposite of you're out.

## **Drunks and drinking**

Drunk: Hey, bartender. Was Billy Brown in here a little while ago?
Bartender: Yes, he was
Drunk: Did you happen to notice if I was with him?

Drunk: Hey, bartender was I in here few hours ago?
Bartender: Yes, you were.
Drunk: Did I leave?
Bartender: Yes, you did.
Drunk: did you happen to notice which way I went?

Does your tongue burn when you drink booze?
I don't know, I never tried to light it.

Here is a great parlor game. Everyone sits around in a circle and drinks a bottle of two-dollar whiskey and tries to guess who they are.

The doctor told him if he didn't quit drinking it would kill him. He put away a six pack of beer and a fifth of whiskey every day. And it killed him. 52 years later he died.

When pink elephants get drunk they see him.

A police officer stopped a man for running a stop sign. The man insisted he did not run a stop sign. The officer insisted he did. His wife who was sitting in the passenger seat said; "Officer you don't want to argue with my husband when he's drinking.

I need glasses. About three of four more of these.

The National Saloon Owner's Association voted him the outdoorsman of the year award. He was thrown out of more doors than anyone in the county.

Thank you for that wooooner-fullll applause (holding in a vomit) lay-dees and gentllmmmm. Laaaay-deeees and gentlmmmm, folks. I am glad to be standing here (burp) heeeer tooooo- nigggght. I am glad to be staaaaaning anywhere tonight. I don't usually walk out in front of an audience when I am this Kon dicheion (condition). I don't usually walk anywhere in the condition. But there is a reason that I am in this connnn- dishhhh (burp) connn dish--un. I have been drinking all day.

Happy new year
What do you mean happy new year? Its April
April? Oh boy, am I in trouble? I haven't been home from the new year's party.

A drunk was standing under a lamp post looking up at the light shouting, "I know you're home, I can see your light on, now open the door.

I wouldn't say he was a drinking man, but when he eats the olive from his martini he thinks that entitles him for an after-dinner drink.

I don't usually come out on stage in this condition. I don't usually go anywhere in this condition. There is a reason I am drunk, tonight. I have been drinking all day. It was a woman that drove me to drink. One of these days I need to remember to write and thank her.


## Dum Dums

If being dumb was an occupation he would be a success

If brains were gun powder he wouldn't have enough to blow his nose

Not everybody has your brains. Some people are sharp,

Working with a wheel barrow has don him a lot of good. He learned to walk on his hind legs.

The guy at the pizza place if he wanted it cut in eight or sixteen pieces. He said eight pieces, I could never eat sixteen pieces of pizza.

If there were 114 people like him, you would have gross ignorance.

I thought he was going to be an astronaut. He took up space in school.

I had an eight-course dinner last night. A baloney sandwich and a six pack.

The other day, I found myself with a piece of rope in my hand. It really caused me some concern. I can't remember if I had lost a horse or found a piece of rope.

He was an accountant who kept hearing strange invoices.

He claims he can't remember who he is. Claims he was found on a door step. Maybe he is a newspaper.

Hey, I may look stupid but that doesn't mean I'm not.

Barren brain

Midget mind

You don't know your own mind. If you did you would hate it.

You will be all right, all you need is a ventriloquist.

He buried his nose in a book and can't remember which book he buried in in.

I thought dum jokes were stupid until I met him.

Even duct tape can't fix stupid, but at least it muffles the sound.

Nineteen Newfoundlanders go to the cinema. The ticket lady asks, "Why so many of you?" Buddy replies, "The film said 18 or over."

My daughter asked me for a pet spider for her birthday. So, I went to our local pet shop and they were $70. Forget it, I thought, I can get one cheaper off the web.

I was at an A.T.M. yesterday. A little old lady asked if I could check her balance, so, I pushed her over.

Statistically, six out of seven dwarfs are not Happy.

My neighbor knocked on my door at 2:30 am. Can you believe that! 2:30 am? Luckily for him I was still up playing my bagpipes.

The wife was counting all the nickels and dimes out on the kitchen table when she suddenly got very angry and started shouting and crying for no reason. I thought to myself, "She's going through the change."

My girlfriend thinks that I'm a stalker. Well, she's not exactly my girlfriend yet.

Sometimes when I close my eyes, I can't see.

Sometimes I think I'm on the right track only to find I am on the wrong train.

## Entertainers

Before he played the piano, he was bothered by his neighbors. Now doesn't have any neighbors.

Now I don't want to brag too much about this comedy team's wit but between the two of them make a half-wit.

Our last show received mixed notices. We liked it, no one else did.

Now, folks there is an announcer for you. He got his start at the Pennsylvania train station.

It took us twelve years to perfect this act. It was a government ob.

This act is really antique. I mean unique,

This act has a happy ending. You will be happy when it's over.

I was in the habit of getting $500 per show. This job cured me of that habit.

NBC wants him, Fox news wants him, Saturday night live wants him, the FBI wants him.

We have just signed a 5-year contract with the management here. We really hooked them. The contract states we agree not to appear for the next five years.

On behalf of the management, I would like to say. . . I would like to be half of the management.

We stole the show.
Somebody should have.

We had the audience glued to their seats.
That was a sneaky way of keeping them there.

Dummy: You'll be alright. All you need is a ventriloquist.

He does one liners because the dummy can't remember two lines,

This next act could possibly be the greatest act in showbusiness. It could be. . . but it ain't

Let's hear a big round of pity for. . .

That was a real mediocre speech harry, keep up the bland work.

I am your second favorite entertainer? Who is first?
(name of animal actor)

I decided I would accept another offer until the time is right. That will be only. . . when some one asks me.

Our humble thanks to those heroic musicians who make our hum-drum lives even more so.

As an actor no one could touch him. As a person no one wants to touch him.

Tonight, our guest star is one that needs no introduction. (look in inside coat pocket pull out paper. Look at paper. Then to audience and read) **Summons to appear**. Oh, (take out another paper read guest's name).

Some Ventriloquist. He throws his voice and the audience keeps throwing it back.

Thank you. You are great audience. I wish I had a better act.

We had a dinner in his honor. Well actually it was a fish fry.

Thank you for attending the dinner tonight. We had planned to have chicken, but it got well.

At every performance there is a line of people
Waiting to get out.

This audience is hungry for entertainment
I think we killed their appetite.

What do you mean? why I have a great delivery.
I know I saw your truck parked outside.

Our back-up band tonight is Ken Carlson and the Carol County Car Strippers.
This is a great job for someone who has never had a nervous breakdown and always wanted one.

I think after this show I may need to learn a trade.

(At a fund raiser where guest pay big money for plate) Hey, If they are paying fifty-bucks a plate why are we doing this for free?

His fan club held a dinner in his honor. Actually, it was fish fry.

Our fan club came to see us when we arrived in town. Well it wasn't the entire fan club only two showed up. One guy was sick and the other had to work.

## Famous People

Today is Abraham Lincoln's birthday. Did you get him anything?

Abraham Lincoln walked twelve miles to return a book. Now they close the library on his birthday. How wrong is that?

Do you know why George Washington stood up in the boat as he crossed the Delaware river? Because every time he sat down somebody handed him an oar.

The other day I re-read the book of Robin Hood. The big deal is he robbed from the rich. Big deal. Of course, he robbed from the rich, the poor had no money.

Our theme song is; we got no business in show business.

Donald Trump had just stepped out from his limousine. His Secret Service officers surrounded as he began walking toward the building. Just then a man stepped out with a rock ready to throw it at the President. A Secret Service officer yelled Mickey Mouse! The perpetrator was so stunned he dropped the rock and the officers grabbed him. "Why did you yell Mickey Mouse when you saw the president was under attack?" asked the supervisor. "This is my first day on the job and I get a bit excited. I didn't mean to say Mickey Mouse, I meant to say Donald duck!

## Flying

A pilot was suspended for thirty days because he walked up the passenger aisle reading a book called "How to Fly in 10 Easy Lessons.

A female flight attendant walked past a passenger who had been drinking heavily. He patted the attendant on her rear end. She said; "Hey watch that mister." He said; "I have been for the past 45 minutes."

I knew we were in for an unusual flight when the pilot came through the cabin taking up a collection for gas.

Do I enjoy flying? I get dizzy when the barber pumps up my chair.

The flight was Okay, until I opened the window.

"Good afternoon ladies and gentlemen. We are about one hour into our flight, so I just wanted to welcome you to flight 407 non-stop to. . . . . . Atlanta. Atlanta? Hey navigator, are sure it says Atlanta?

Has anyone ever flown to Atlanta before? You have sir? Would you recognize it from the air?

## Food - Restaurants

The hotdog is the only animal in the world that feeds the hand that bites it.

I made a shoo-fly pie for the party. I was going to make a sponge cake, but I couldn't find the right kind of sponge.

Waiter: How did you find the steak sir?
Diner: Oh, I just moved a few peas and there it was.

If we had some donuts we could have coffee and donuts if we had the coffee.

I used to brag about carrying twenty dollars' worth of food in one hand, now days I can carry twenty dollars of food in my pocket. You know, I think its cheaper to eat money.

Is the coffee done?
It should be its been cookin' since last Tuesday.

Oh, it's fresh. It has been fresh for six months.

Diner: Waiter, do you expect me to eat this slop? Call the manager.
Waiter: That's no-good sir, he won't eat it either.

The best way to make Mexican chilly is pout ice water down his back.

Here is a little health tip for you. If you want to stay healthy remember, an apple a day keeps the doctor away. An onion a day keeps everyone away.

This stuff will make you thick to your stomach.

Yes, I would be glad to attend. If the dinner is free and the dinner's not me, I'll be there.

We were going to serve chicken for dinner tonight, but it got well.

It's not good for you to eat on my empty stomach.

I had a terrible dream last night!  I dreamed I was at a banquet and there were a thousand different kinds of food to eat and I wasn't hungry!

A hot dog is the only animal in the world that feed the hand that bites it!

I was going to make a sponge cake, but I couldn't find a sponge.

Want to join me in a bowl of soup?  Only if you get in first!

The best way to make Mexican chili is to pour ice water down his back!

Why don't you join me for dinner....at your house!?

Why don't you come over for dinner...? if you don't mind imposing.

How did you find the steak, sir?  Oh, I just moved a few peas and there it was!

Waiter, how do you expect me to eat this stuff?  Call the manager!  It's no use sir, he won't eat it either!

If we had some donuts we could have coffee and donuts!  If we had some coffee!

Coffee hot?  Should be, it's been cooking since last Thursday!

That meat is fresh.  Been fresh for six months!

An apple a day keeps the doctor away.  An onion a day keeps everybody away!

That stuff will make you thick to your stomach!

The steaks were the size of manhole covers!  And they even tasted like manhole covers!

If the dinner is free and the dinner's not me, tell them I'll be there!

You will never forget your birthday, if my wife bakes the cake.

I won't say she is a bad cook, but, we have the only mice in town receiving meals on wheels.

I'm no cook, I am a direction reader.

That caviar has a fishy taste.

Due to circumstances beyond our control. . . dinner is now being served.

I won't say the food in that restaurant was bad, but I noticed everyone order Alka-Seltzer for desert.


Is this coffee, tea or what?
What does it taste like?
Gasoline.
It's tea, the coffee tastes like dishwater.

The last steak I had, I cut it out of a magazine.

The waiter called it a three-minute steak. He was right. It took me 3 minutes to find it.

How did you find your steak sir?
Oh, I just moved a few peas and there it was.

Where is my waiter?
He went to lunch, sir.
Lunch?
You don't expect him to eat in this joint, do you?

I guess by now you know the dinner will be late. The cook is sick. We told him not to eat here.

Hi, pal, sit down and have a drink on me. Waiter, bring my friend a glass of water.

We had lunch at one of these sidewalk cafes. It started to rain. It took me an hour to finish my soup.

I'll have a waitress, no dressing.

This place has some kitchen. When the health department has to send an inspector out, they ask for volunteers.

Waiter. There is a fly in my soup.
Not so loud every-body will want on.

Waiter. There is a fly in my soup. What is this fly doing in my soup?
Looks a back stroke to me.

Waiter what is the meaning of this.
The meaning of what, sir?
What is the meaning of this fly swimming in my soup.
It means you have too much soup. He should be wading.

Diner walking out of restaurant. A bowl falls out from under his coat. "Okay who threw that?"

She can't cook minute rice in under an hour.

They said it was blended coffee. Yeah, they blended yesterdays with today's

He finished an 18-day diet in five days. Claims he's a fast eater.

I gained twenty pounds on Neutra-system. Who knew that box was supposed to last 30-days.

Waiter what is this fly doing in my soup?
It looks like he is dying of ptomaine poisoning.

Day one of my diet instructions said clear all the bad food from your house. I did. It was delicious.

## Funny Love Lines

Do you still love me? Are you still rich? Answer the second question first.

Just say you'll marry me and you'll never see me again.

Let's go into the living room and start living.

How did you learn to kiss like that?
I used to play a trumpet.

Come up to my apartment and we will toast the new year.
The new year is still 7 months away.
You don't have to leave, early do you?

Tell me about yourself. Your hopes, your dreams, your cell phone number.

Come up to my room. I want to hate myself in the morning.

If nobody claims me in 30 days, I'm yours.

Please, your steaming up my glasses.

One kiss from her and you will not want to waste your lips on eating again.

So, you think you have pretty lips? Why, I'd put mine up against yours anytime.

How do you keep a figure like that?
Oh, I don't pay any attention to it.
You don't know what you're missing.

Oh, I'm just a woman.
I know, but you are so good at it.

Everything about you reminds me of you.

I could not have happened to a nicer girl.

Good morning handsome.
It was beautiful, but now it is sensational.

O.K. meet me in the garden next to the scarecrow. You better wear a ribbon, so I will recognize You.

Dancing is just hugging set to music.
What don't you like about that?
The music.

What is your name?
Jane.
Jane? Can I call you Jane? When Jane?

Boy, that was quick. You don't fool around do you? Do you?

What do you mean it didn't work out as well as I said it would? Did you tell her that her beauty would make time stand still?
Well not exactly in those words, but the meaning was the same.
What did you say?
I said, Baby your face could stop a clock.

## Gambling

Lady Godiva put all she had on a horse.

No, I don't object to nine aces in a deck of cards. But he has five and I dealt myself four, well. . .

Well, there's plenty more where that money went.

Oh, aid you. I thought you said fade you.

He played 21 all night. He didn't get a blackjack until he got to the parking lot.

## Golf

I just discovered something that took ten points off my game. It's called an eraser.

Have you noticed how carts are taking the place of the caddy? Let's face it, they have three distinct advantages; They don't charge, they don't criticize, and they don't count strokes.

Life is like one big golf tournament. As soon as you get out of one hole, you head for another.

I play golf, right away you know two important things about me; I may be a liar but at least I am a gentleman.

Golf! Now there is a good walk spoiled.

The closest I ever came to a hole in one is a six.

I don't need a caddy, I need a compass.

I have found the most difficult part of golf is getting out of the house to play it.

He plays a fair game of golf. If you watch him.

## Homes and houses

They are going to tear it down and build slums.

I won' say she is a lousy house keeper, but their dog buried his bone in their living room rug.

We have a swimming pool in the front yard. We call it a swimming pool. The city calls it a clogged sewer.

Va Va Voom what a room

People who live in glass houses shouldn't throw stones, or wild parties.

I live so far out the mail man mails me my mail.

What a great view. On a clear day you can see the Pacific Ocean. On a windy day you are in it/

They gave us the key to the city. Next month they are going to erect a slum in our honor.

When I left home my Mom said she would leave a light on for me. I came home after two years and she welcomed me home with a big dinner and a gas bill for $455.

A beautiful house in the suburbs surrounded by mortgages.

I bought a hose by the lake. Now I am surrounded with pests; mosquitoes, ants, uncles, and cousins.


## Horses

The most observant man in the world is the guy who noticed Lady Godiva had a horse with her.

The horse took so long to come in, the jockey had a change of saddle.

Photo finish, not this horse. A painting, maybe!

This was a race for five-year olds. What some parents won't do for money.

The track had a $5 window and a $1.98 for women.

No, no a horse cannot be man's best friend like a dog. How would you like to have a horse jump up into your lap?

Ahhh, Kentucky. Land of beautiful horses and fast women.

## Hotels – motels

The owners call it the Biltmore. If you ask me, it is Biltmore (built more) like a stable.

It was a nice quiet little hotel just forty-five minutes from the city. . . by telephone.

The room was so small I didn't have room to change my mind.

Oh, it was an exclusive hotel. Room service had an unlisted number.

The sign on the gate to the pool said: "Swim at your own risk, the lifeguard didn't get the raise he asked for."

Small room? I guess you could say it was a small room. When I open the door, the light comes on. Every time I smile my teeth touch the walls.

We played in some of the leading resorts in Florida. We did our act a few of the too.

My room has an adjoining. An adjoining what I don't know, I can't get that door open.

Run down? Well, let's put it this way. They had to clean it up before the health department would come in to condemn it.

Conrad Hilton wept here.

Remind me not to go back there on my next vacation.

He bragged about its strong foundation and rugged construction. So, is a pyramid but who wants to live in one?

Air conditioned? Oh, yeah, I never seen air in such a condition.

We stayed at the Opryland Hotel in Nashville. Now. There is a large hotel. They are thinking about applying for statehood.


## Husbands

He's not husband he is a has been.

Your husband is not dead lady, he's hiding.

It must be tough living with a woman stupid enough to marry you.

**Insults** (a gag for people who are interrupting your act or when you just need an insult)

Have you ever considered lacing up your mouth and renting your head out for football?

If anyone asks me what I see in You what can I tell them?

Yes, I am enjoying myself, there is nobody else to enjoy on this show.

Yes, medicine breath.

He is the sap in the family tree.

You couldn't draw a crowd if you were a gutter on New Year's Eve.

He wasn't born, he was squeezed out of a bar rag.

Today is his birthday. This time 20 years ago his father was seen throwing rocks at the stork.

He has a half horsepower brain pushing a ten-ton mouth.

His breath is offensive. It keeps him alive.

You should lose your temper. The one you got now is terrible.

Have you ever thought of changing your mind? The one you got now doesn't work too good.

Touchy? This guy is a walking land mine.

We were just talking about chipping in and buying you a smile.

I taught him everything he knows. Roll over, play dead, fetch. . .

Why don't you bore a hole in your head and let the sap run out?

Ugly? When snakes get drunk they see him.

Look at that, would you. The last time I saw anything like that I had to pay admission.

The missing tooth in the smile of victory

Hating him is so good, there should be a luxury tax on it.

He is like air in a pet shop.

Can I borrow your IQ? I'm going to a masquerade party as a moron.

You have a charming way of never saying anything intelligent.

You know, you have that certain. . . nothing.

Say, are you the guy that invented the tooth ache?

Why don't you take a ride on a leaky submarine?

If you are looking for entertainment, don't look at me, I am ventriloquist not an animal trainer.

What a waste of skin.

Are those your knees or are you smuggling walnuts?

Is that your ears or are you a model for ping pong paddles?

He is a regular one-man slum.

If you cross him with an ape, you would get a retarded ape.

They were sitting around in a circle, it looked like a dope ring.

You talk about a guy with no friends, his obituary was printed under neighborhood improvement.

Now, now don't compare him to an ape. At least he peels the banana before he eats it.

To him a cookout is a fire in a garbage can.

They don't let him swim in the city swimming pool any more, he leaves an oil slick.

They don't let him swim in the lake anymore he leaves a ring around the pier.

After he took a bath they had to dredge the tub.

He took a five-minute coffee break and had to be retrained.

I won't say he is out of touch, but he had to study for a blood test.

There is only two reasons why someone does not mind their own business, either they don't have any business or they haven't any mind.

Hey, if they put a price on your head, take it.

He calls himself an entertainer, why, he couldn't draw crowd if he was a gutter on New Year's Eve.

He is cultured, he can bore you on any subject.

There he is folks, Brittan's answer to Bunker Hill.

What do you mean I don't like you? Why, I worship the ground I wish you were buried under?

What scares me is that sometimes I actually catch myself enjoying you.

If beauty was intoxicating, you would be a whiskey sour.

He is the onion in the breath of life.

Someone told him to act like a movie star, He took their advice. His case comes up next week.

Some people say (name) dyes his hair brown. That is not true. It was already brown when he bought it.

He knows a great deal about nothing and nothing about a great deal.

If baloney were snow, you would be blizzard.

The last time I saw something like him I pinned a tail on it. (pin the tail on the donkey game)

I don't know where you were before I met you but wish you would go back there.

I can explain it to you, but I can't understand it for you.

After listening to you for a while, I ask myself, who ties your shoe laces for you?

You are confusing my personality with my attitude. My personality is who I am, my attitude depends on who you are.

Just because your head comes to a point that doesn't mean you're sharp.

Hey, I haven't seen a face like that since I gave up drinking.

O. K. you, put on your shoes and out.

Why don't you bore a hole in your head and let the sap run out.

Can I have your head, I'm starting a rock collection.

When I Look at you I get tremendous desire to be lonesome.

Would you mind closing the door, from the outside.

Haven't I seen your face on a bottle of poison?

You would make a wonderful model for totem poles.

I would like to help you out. Which way did you come in?

I would like to see you get ahead. You need one.

Have you ever considered lacing up your mouth and renting yourself out as a football?

If anyone asked me what I see in you, what can I tell them?

They say no man really knows himself. That certainly makes you the lucky one.

He has a half horse power brain driving a 10-ton mouth.

Touchy? This guy is a walking land mine.

He thinks he's an idiot. Talk about conceited.

(Short person) Are you comfortable sitting there? Do you need another phone book?

(short person) Hey, look great. It looks like you took off some. . . height.

We were just talking about chipping in and buying you a smile.

Now he has finally made it, and can live high on the hog, and the Rabbi won't let him eat pork.

The say people think of you as (something here) that's not true, nobody thinks of you at all.

(well-known person in audience) is over there explain the jokes to (another well-known person in audience)

I taught him everything he knows. Roll over, sit up, speak, play dead.

I think he was the first one born in captivity.

He was the teacher's pet. Literally.


## Irish Jokes

Paddy was driving down the street in a sweat because he had an important meeting and couldn't find a parking place.   Looking up to heaven he said, 'Lord take pity on me.   If you find me a parking place I will go to Mass every Sunday for the rest of me life and give up me Irish Whiskey!'

Miraculously, a parking place appeared.

Paddy looked up again and said, 'Never mind, I found one Father Murphy walks into a pub in Donegal, and asks the first man he meets, 'Do you want to go to heaven?'

The man said, 'I do, Father...'

The priest said, 'Then stand over there against the wall.'

Then the priest asked the second man, 'Do you want to go to heaven?'

'Certainly, Father,' the man replied.

'Then stand over there against the wall,' said the priest.

Then Father Murphy walked up to O'Toole and asked, 'Do you want to go to heaven?'

O'Toole said, 'No, I don't Father.'

The priest said, 'I don't believe this.   You mean to tell me that when you die you don't want to go to heaven?'

O'Toole said, 'Oh, when I die, yes.   I thought you were getting a group together to go right now.'

Paddy was in New York patiently waiting and watching the traffic cop on a busy street crossing.   The cop stopped the flow of traffic and shouted, 'Okay, pedestrians.'   Then he'd allow the traffic to pass.

He'd done this several times, and Paddy still stood on the sidewalk.

After the cop had shouted, 'Pedestrians!' for the tenth time, Paddy went over to him and said, 'Is it not about time ye let the Catholics across?'

Gallagher opened the morning newspaper and was dumbfounded to read in the obituary column that he had died.   He quickly phoned his best friend, Finney. 'Did you see the paper?' asked Gallagher. 'They say I died!!'

'Yes, I saw it!' replied Finney.   'Where are ye callin' from?'

An Irish priest is driving down to New York and gets stopped for speeding in Connecticut.   The state trooper smells alcohol on the priest's breath and then sees an empty wine bottle on the floor of the car.

He says, 'Sir, have you been drinking?'

'Just water,' says the priest.

The trooper says, 'Then why do I smell wine?'

The priest looks at the bottle and says, 'Good Lord! He's done it again!'

Walking into the bar, Mike said to Charlie the bartender, 'Pour me a stiff one - just had another fight with the little woman.'

'Oh yeah?' said Charlie, 'And how did this one end?'

'When it was over,' Mike replied, 'She came to me on her hands and knees.'

'Really,' said Charles, 'Now that's a switch!   What did she say?'

She said, 'Come out from under the bed, you little chicken.'

David staggered home very late after another evening with his drinking buddy, Paddy.   He took off his shoes to avoid waking his wife, Kathleen.

He tiptoed as quietly as he could toward the stairs leading to their upstairs bedroom but misjudged the bottom step.   As he caught himself by grabbing the banister, his body swung around, and he landed heavily on his rump.   A whiskey bottle in each back pocket broke and made the landing especially painful.

Managing not to yell, David sprung up, pulled down his pants, and looked in the hall mirror to see that his butt cheeks were cut and bleeding.   He managed to quietly find a full box of Band-Aids and began putting a Band-Aid as best he could on each place he saw blood.

He then hid the now almost empty Band-Aid box and shuffled and stumbled his way to bed.  In the morning, David woke up with searing pain in both his head and butt and Kathleen staring at him from across the room. She said, 'You were drunk again last night, weren't you?'

David said, 'Why you say such a mean thing?'

'Well,' Kathleen said, 'it could be the open front door, it could be the broken glass at the bottom of the stairs, it could be the drops of blood trailing through the house, it could be your bloodshot eyes, but mostly ...... it's all those Band-Aids stuck on the hall mirror.

## Losers

He was on the golf course trying to improve his game. While he practiced keeping his head down he was hit by a golf ball.

Life is a hard row to hoe and he doesn't have a hoe.

He used saccharine instead of sugar and came down with artificial diabetes.

He wanted a tattoo but didn't like the idea of putting ink under his skin. The tattoo artist said he could use colored water with sugar to give it some texture. It looked good for a while until he came down with tattoo diabetes.

When his bookie's place burned down the only thing the firemen saved was his I O Us.

What a loser. Some people just can't get a break. He found a summons in a fortune cookie.

He bought a set of snow tires. . . and they melted.

Ok, who put the tranquilizers in the cheese dip?

A black cat crossed his path and the cat had seven years bad luck.

Walked under a black cat and seven years of ugly mirrors.

Someone sent his picture to Ripley's Believe it or Not. They sent it back, they didn't believe it.

He tried turning over a new leaf but that turned out to be poison ivy.

I have decided I am tired of chasing my dreams. I'm just going to ask where they are going and I will meet them there.


## Love and Marriage

It takes two to make a marriage. A young girl and her anxious mother

We were married by a judge. I should have asked for a jury.

The groom is a fella who spends a great deal on a suit that nobody notices.

Bigamy is having more than one mother-in-law.

So, you are worried about me giving up single bliss for the old ball and chain. Have you seen her? It will be a ball being chained to her.

Do you want to know why the cost of divorce is so expensive? Because it's worth it!


I told her I was going to be the master of my house or I'll know the reason why.
What did she say to that?
Well, let's put it this way. I know the reason why.


I am going to marry an ugly girl.
Why don't want to marry a beautiful girl?
Because a beautify girl might run away.
An ugly girl can run too you know.
Yeah but who cares?

I remember the first time I kissed her. Our lips just seemed to stick together. I told her to spit out her gum but oh no.


Sure, I love you. Say you'll marry me and you'll never see me again.


Every man needs a wife. Just think of all the things that happen that you can't blame on the government.


It's the little things that break up a marriage. Little blondes, little red heads, little brunettes.
Love and Marriage

IK told her I would make her happy if it took every dollar he father has.

He told her that if she didn't marry him he would die. She didn't and sure enough 35 years later he died.

She's a gorgeous creature. And not a bad looking girl either.

I heard it said that one day men will wake up and find the world run by women. Now isn't that just like a woman, taking advantage of a guy while he is asleep.

If you don't marry me I will hang myself on your front porch.
Now, you know my dad does not want you hanging around here.

Say those three little words that will set my feet on air.
Go hang yourself.

They say two can live as cheaply as one. But who wants to live cheaply?

I hear married men live longer.  I don't think so, it just seems longer

I went to city hall to see when my marriage license expired

I was married by a judge. I should have asked for a jury.

He just took his first step toward divorce. He got married.

Marriage is like a poker game. You start with a pair, He shows his heart, then flashes a diamond. She shows a flush and before long you have a full house,

A wife is a wonderful thing. She will stick by you through all the problems you would not have if you had not married her in the first place.

I am only going to marry an ugly girl.
Why an ugly girl?
Because a beautiful girl may run away.
An ugly girl can run too, you know/
Yeah, but who cares?

Where did you learn to kiss like that?
I used to play a trombone.

Marriage is like a cafeteria. You go in, look over the possibilities, select what you like and pay later.

A bride groom is a person who spends a lot of money on a suit that nobody notices.

A little 6-year-old little girl was attending a wedding ceremony for the first time. "Why is the lady wearing a white dress?" She asked her grandmother.
"White is the color for happiness," she answered. This is the happiest day of her life."
After a few minutes the little, looking confused, asked. "Why is the man wearing all black?"

## Master of Ceremonies lines

Good ladies evening and gentlemen. Ah oh I mean good evening ladies and gentlemen. I can see right now what kind of night this is going to be.

Here is a message for ah Mister and Mrs. Smith. (reading from note) it is from your baby sitter. She wants to know . . . where your . . . (turn paper over) fire extinguisher is.

After this next act, there will be ten-minute intermission while someone opens a window.

I would like to say that this next act is one of the top billing acts in the country. I would like to say that, but I am not that big a liar.

This next act has been on television, this act has been on stage this is probably the biggest has been act in the business.

This act has wowed audiences in Las Vegas, this act has wowed audiences on television. This is the wowziest act in the business.

Here they are, direct from the bar (name act)

This next act has been sweeping the country, and after you see them you will have to admit that is where they belong, out in the country sweeping.

Thank you for that speech, John, it was really mediocre, keep up the bland work.

(after beautiful girl act) Thank you (look at girl walking off} Fella.

We can M. C. a talent show, with-out a conflict of interest.

He is a great man around town, he has told me that time and again.

I was over there explaining the jokes to (name of person in the audience everyone knows)

He is an outstanding personality. Not you (person audience knows) If you could stand up you have been gone hours ago.

(to short person) How are you doing (name) are you enjoying yourself? Do you need another book to sit on?

Some entertainer, he can't even entertain a thought.

This next act has been around for a long time. They used to follow a dinosaur act.

Good ladies evening and gentlemen

Here is a message for Mister and Mrs. Smith. (reading) ah, it's from your . . .baby sitter. She . . wants to know. . . where . . . you fire extinguisher is.

Joke flops: (remove paper from pocket. Pretend to write on it while saying to yourself) "Fire Joke writer."

He is really popular. Several TV shows wants him, the FBI wants him.

After this next act there will be a ten-minute intermission for someone to open the windows.

I would like to say that this next act is the best in the business. I's like to say how much I enjoy this act. I would like to say that but I'm not that big a liar

This act has wowed audiences in Los Angeles, they have wowed audiences in Las Vegas, they have wowed audiences in New York. I guess you could say this is the wow-z iest act in the business.

Here they are. . . direct from the bar. . .

This next act has been sweeping the country and after you see them you will agree that is exactly what they should be doing. . .  out in the country sweeping.

## Men (some of these can be used as M.C. lines)

He is the most honest man money can buy.

He is as honest as the day is long . . .  in the winter . . . in the Artic

When he coins a phrase, its counterfeit.

He likes the night life. Owls, rodents, bats

I heard you were sick. If I were you I would be sick too.

He could be worse. He could be twins.

He is a man of convictions and they are all for D U I.

He lived in the same house for almost 20 years. Then the governor pardoned him.

He's a nice guy. He owns a newspaper. He doesn't read it he just carries it around with him.

Talk about tight, He has a one-way wallet.

His right eye is beautiful. So beautiful in fact his left eye keeps looking at it.

I told him to treat my house as though it was his own. Yesterday he sold it.

He is the reason hotels have security cameras.

He just bought a new yacht. The old one got wet.

He is a big banker. Just yesterday he banked a three ball in the side pocket,

He passed a black cat and the cat had 7 years bad luck.

He walked under a black cat and had 7 years of ugly mirrors.

You know what I like about him? Nothin'

He shaves with an electric razor. He doesn't trust himself in front of a mirror with a razorblade in his hand.

Looks are deceiving. He is not really dead.

He is a man of steal.

He is the most honest man money can buy.

He is honest as the day is long. In the winter. . . in the artic.

He has a drinking problem. I can drink more than he can afford.

He likes the night life. Owls, rodents, bats.

He is worth a million dollars. In confederate money.

He could be worse. He could be twins.

Adam was a pollack. Who else could eat an apple from of a naked lady?

He is a man of convictions.  They are both for D U I.

Who could fill his shoes? It would take 3 shovels full.

His secret is long hours, hard work, and a total disregard for quality.

There he is folks, two hundred and fifty pounds of silly putty.

His motto is good grief.

He has all the charm of an impacted wisdom tooth.

Have you ever thought of gluing your tongue down?

Talk about a hypochondriac! He gargles just to see if his throat leaks.

He is a little worried. He took his annual insurance physical the other day and today is insurance company took their calendar back.

Talk about lazy. He is the kind of guy that gets into a revolving door and waits.

The most observant man in history is the guy that noticed Lady Godiva had a horse with her.

Ugly, sleep stays away from him 'till he covers his face.

He entered the Mister America contest and lost his citizenship.


## Money

One: He must be rich. He flies his own twin engine airplane.
Two: So?
One: In his living room?

I was living in the lap of luxury, then luxury stood up.

The Internal Revenue is the world's most successful mail order business.

Rich? H bought a new yacht because the old on got wet.

This guy is so rich, that when he takes a bath it leaves a 14-karat ring around the tub.

I couldn't afford to get life insurance, so I went down to the local finance company and borrowed ten thousand dollars. They will not let anything happen to me.

I would give a thousand dollars to be a millionaire.

Ten years ago, I dreamed of making the money I am starving on today.

His family's coat of arms has two pair of pants.

I'm not worried about money. Yesterday I lit my cigar with a hundred dollar bill. I think it was my electric bill.

I'll tell ya what keeps me out of the stock market, the supermarket that's what.


Money is what things run into and people run out of.

Money is what you use when you can't find your credit card.

What do you mean brief case? That's his wallet.

Remember when charity was a virtue instead of an industry?

No one knows what I have gone through, except maybe the tellers at the First National Bank.

I spent the holidays with one of the world's biggest spenders. My wife.

Well, there's plenty more where that went.

Don't you wish the man who does the bank commercials was the one who makes the loans?

This guy doesn't count his money, he measures it!

Some people spend all their lies doing something they hate to make money they don't want to buy things they can't afford to impress people they don't like.

Money can't buy happiness, but it can sure put you into a wonderful bargaining position.

What this country needs is a good five cent nickel.

Oh, go read your money

I am just a care free guy. I don't care as long as it's free.

What do you mean a dollar doesn't go far these days? Did you ever try to get one back?


## Movies

Today, if you identify with a movie hero, you're sick

What a movie! It was so good some of the lovers in the audience were actually watching it.

I won't say it was a bad movie, but I understand six states are using it as capital punishment.

When it comes to acting, Busty Heartburn (actress with big breasts) is way out in front.

That movie was the greatest think since dark balconies.

## Music

Dummy: Let's sing the one I just rottened.

Vent: rottened. You don't rotten a song. It is written

Dummy: Well you ain't heard it yet.

## News Papers

The town's editor of the obituary column has retired. His son has taken over the column. Starting tomorrow, the one completing this segment of the newspaper will be the son of obituary editor.

Want Add: Lion tamer wants tamer lion.

Want Add: 1926 Mercedes for sale, take over payments.

Local News: Used car dealer gets robbed.

He owns a newspaper. He doesn't read it he just carries it around.


## Old Folks

When is this old enough to know better kick in?

I am not really a grouchy old man. I am just at the age where I will stop being civil and start being myself.

An old woman walked up and tied her old mule to the hitching post. As she stood there, brushing some of the dust from her face and clothes, a young gunslinger stepped out of the saloon with a gun in one hand and a bottle of whiskey in the other. the young gunslinger looked at the old woman and laughed, "hey old woman, have you ever danced?"

the old woman looked up at the gunslinger and said, "no,... i never did dance... never really wanted to."

A crowd had gathered as the gunslinger grinned and said "well, you old bag, you're gonna dance now," and started shooting at the old woman's feet. The old woman prospector -- not wanting to get her toe blown off --started hopping around. everybody was laughing. when his last bullet had been fired, the young gunslinger, still laughing, holstered his gun and turned around to go back into the saloon. The old woman turned to her pack mule, pulled out a double-barreled shotgun, and cocked both hammers. the loud clicks carried clearly through the desert air, and the crowd stopped laughing immediately. The young gunslinger heard the sounds, too, and he turned around very slowly. the silence was almost deafening. the crowd watched as the young gunman stared at the old woman and the large gaping holes of those twin barrels. The barrels of the shotgun never wavered in the old woman's hands, as she quietly said, "son, have you ever kissed a mule's ass?"

The gunslinger swallowed hard and said, "no m'am... but i've always wanted to.

there are five lessons here for all of us:

1 - never be arrogant.

2 - don't waste ammunition.

3 - whiskey makes you think you're smarter than you are.

4 - always make sure you know who has the power.

5 - don't mess with old people; they didn't get old by being stupid.

Two guys grow up together but after college one moves to Michigan, the other to Florida. They agree to meet every ten years in Vero Beach to play golf.

At age 30, they finish their round of golf and go to lunch.

"Where you wanna go?"

"Hooters."

"Why?"

"Well, you know, they got the broads, with the big racks, and the tight shorts, and the legs ..."

"OK."

Ten years later at age 40 they meet and play again.

"Where you wanna go?"

"Hooters.

"Why?"

"Well, you know, they got cold beer and the big screen TVs and everybody has a little action on the games."

"OK."

Ten years later at age 50 they meet and play again. "Where you wanna go?"

"Hooters."

"Why?"

"The food is pretty good and there is plenty of parking."

"OK."

At age 60 they meet and play again.

"Where you wanna go?"

"Hooters."

"Why?"

"Wings are half price."

"OK"

At age 70 they meet and play again.
"Where you wanna go?"

"Hooters."

"Why?"

"They have 6 handicapped spaces right by the door."

"OK."

At age 80 they meet and play again.
"Where you wanna go?"

"Hooters."

"Why?"
"We've never been there before."


## Poetry

I think I shall never hear a poem lovelier than a beer
The brew that joe's bar has on tap with golden base and snowy cap
The foamy stuff I drink all day until my memories melt away
Poems are made by fools I fear, but only Bud can make a beer. (use any brand name)

Don't make love at the garden gate.

Because love is blind but the neighbors aint.

Twenty-five children had Mrs. O'Brien

She feels fine, but the stork is dying.

Just think how long a tall giraffe, would take to have a belly laugh.

A limerick produces a laugh agnomical

In a space that is most economical

But good I've seen are seldom clean

And the clean ones not very comical.

## School

I am next to the smartest guy in school. He sits beside me.

I am doing must better in Algebra. I can almost sleep through the whole class.

In school I sang in the choir. My voice was so high I had to sing with the girls. By the time I started to enjoy it, my voice changed.

Well, I have been out of school for many years, and yesterday was another day spent without using algebra.


## Sales people

I am tied with the company's leading salesman. He hasn't sold anything either.

There is an old legend written on the men's room wall at a small hotel in Huston. Salesmen who cover chair instead of territory always on bottom.

I am the second-best salesperson in the company. Of course, there are 180 others tied for first.

All orders signed with a swizzle stick will not accepted.

To be tops in sales you must use your imagination. You know what imagination is, that's what you put into your expense account.

He is one tough sales manager. His e-mails begin with "Now fear this."

I am need improve my sales. If I don't start making money soon, I will have to learn a trade.

He was some salesperson. It will take a lot to fill his shoes. At least four shovels full.

Our secret? Long hours, hard work and a total disregard for quality.

You want to see our sales chart hit an all-time high? Turn it upside down.


## Seasons

I love May. A time when the flowers come up and heat bill goes down.

Well, winter is gone, and spring is here. I know because my neighbor just returned my snow blower and borrowed my lawn mower.

Thirty days hath September, April, June and November. All the rest have 31. Now, do you cll that fair?

I gave up my New Year's resolutions for Lent.

Hot travels faster than cold. You can catch cold.

I love May and June, and April and their other two sisters.

## Sick Jokes

*Sick jokes are not about sickness they are jokes that come from a cleaver, witty but sick mind.*

Are you the young man who saved my little boy when he fell through the ice?
Yes mam, I am
Well where's his mittens?

I don't know if this is tomato juice, or what but I think it is starting to clot.

If you fall off that and break your leg don't come running to me.

This guy is so short, he could milk a cow standing up.

My therapist told me to write letters to all those I consider my enemies, them burn them. The next time I see my therapist I am going to ask him what he wants me to do with the letters.

## Women

**In some cases, these same jokes can be used using a man as reference or for any character you make up. Usually a fictitious character works better.**

Girl with a dog: There goes man's best friend. And she has a dog with her.

She has trouble getting a chest X-ray. She can't get close enough to the machine.

If that low-cut gown slips, it will turn an attraction into a sensation.

Some guy stole my car. I haven't reported it to the police yet. My mother-in-law was sleeping In the back seat. I figure when she wakes up he will glad to return it.

She has a million- dollar figure. Too bad some of it is counterfeit.

She brags about her hour glass figure. Someone should tell her its later than she thinks.

She's a tough one. She works with a blacksmith. When the shoes are ready she hands him the horse.

Getting a chest X-ray is not easy. She can't get close enough to the machine.

If that low-cut gown slips it will turn an attraction into a sensation.

Men do make passes at girls who wear glasses, but it depends on the frame.

She has the right combination to unlock my heart. 36-24-36.

Oh, she's smart. She thinks like the government. She never lets debt keep her from spending more.

Venus De Milo. Can you imagine a body like that and no arms to defend it with?

That dress kept everybody warm but herself.

If you ever watched the golden globe awards, you can understand why TV is called the Boob tube.

That girl is so healthy I get tired just looking at her.

I think, maybe, it is a good thing I don't understand women. Women understand women and they don't like them.

Don't tell me women have no character. They have a new one every day.

We took a long weekend at the beach. Ah, I remember it well. We swam in the water, I buried her in the sand . . . You know, one of these days I may need to go back to that beach and dig her up.

How do you keep a figure like that?
Oh, I don't pay any attention to it.
Well you should, you don't know what you are missing.

My, girl, Sal. Lovely lady. She's a blonde. . . this week.

Oh, I don't think she's tough. You want to know to soften her up? Soak her in money.

Women are like buses. Another will come along any minute.
Yes, but with both you have to have your money ready if you expect to get anywhere.

I have a way with women. No matter how hard they struggle I can always manage to wrap myself around their little finger.

Not attractive? well, no. But I can tell you sleep stays away from her until she covers her face.

Every time she undresses, the man across the street pulls down his blinds.

She entered the Miss America contest and darn near lost her citizenship.

She is a large lady. Every step she takes is recorded by the North China seismograph.

I have heard that women in Bikini swimsuits look shorter. That may be true, but it sure makes men look longer.

A girl who swears she has never been kissed, has a right to swear.

She has more curves than a roller coaster.

Yes, and they both leave you breathless.

So, you like girls, I gather.
I like girls anybody gathers.

You like her I.Q?
I like her whole alphabet.

I hear she is very intellectual and well educated. When you are together what do you talk about?
Who talks?

Oh, it's not hard to meet a girl like her. Just open your wallet.

As soon as you lose your capitol she loses her interest.

Oh, she knows what to give a man who has everything. Encouragement

She's in vogue from the neck down and vague from the neck up.

That evening gown kept everybody warm except her.

Talk about buck teeth, she can eat an apple through a tennis racquet.

Aren't you too young to be trusted with a figure like that?

She's out in the car. In the trunk.

It doesn't take much to soften her up. Just soak her in money.

Ventriloquist: your girlfriend is here? Where is she?

Dummy: see that beautiful girl in the second row, with the, lovely blue eyes, gorgeous figure and
silky blonde hair?

Ventriloquist: Yeah.

Dummy: My girl is the one sitting beside her.

She went to get a chest x-ray, but she couldn't get close enough to the machine.

(Girl with a dog) there goes man's best friend. And she has a dog with her.

Oh, yeah. She has everything a man could want. Lots of money.

She is like a beautiful flower. Surrounded by dirt.

She just had her coming out party. They let her out for good behavior.

She just had a coming out party for her. They chased her back in.

You have heard the old adage, men never make passes at girls who wear glasses. Well it depends on the frame.

She has a million-dollar figure but most of it is counterfeit.

I have a way with women. No matter how hard the struggle I can always manage to wrap my self around her little finger.

They say beauty is only skin deep. That's OK with me, I'm no cannibal.

He takes her every where he goes. He claims it's better than kissing her goodnight.

He told me her beauty could make time stand still. Well, I can tell that face could stop a clock!

Well, lets put it this way. She could be a test pilot for a broom factory.

And the bags under her eyes, I thought her nose was wearing a saddle.

What do you mean she should use more make up? She doesn't need makeup she needs and overhaul.

Talk about different she doesn't say hello, she says boo!
And buck teeth? She can eat an apple through a tennis racquet.

I sent her picture to Ripley's Believe it or Not. They sent it back they didn't believe it!

You can't miss her. She is standing on a bare spot on the ground. Where Zelda goes, nothing grows.

## Wives

He says his wife is as pretty as a picture, Last night he tried to hang her.

He keeps calling her angel. Last night he tried to arrange it.

My wife is a cleaning addict. She is always cleaning. Yesterday she found a thirty five year old bottle of scotch and she threw it away. She thought it was stale.

I spent the holidays with one of the world's biggest spenders. My wife.

My wife finally got around to spring cleaning yesterday. The first thing she did was throw out the Christmas tree.

A wife is a wonderful thing. She will stick by you through all the troubles you would not have had if you hadn't married her in the first place.

You really need a wife, just think of all the things that happen to you that you can't blame on the government.

Do you know what to give a woman who has everything? A husband who can pay for it.

We were walking in the park past a wishing well. My wife looked into it and fell in. I didn't know those things worked!

But, hey, all things considered I have to hand it to my wife. She will get it anyway.

You know you are getting old when you don't care where your wife goes as long as you don't have to go with her.

It must be tough being married to a woman who is crazy enough to marry you.

I told her just how things were going to be from now on. Then I didn't see her for a week. After a week I could barely see her out of my left eye.

She drives a vehicle that gets $200 to the mile. A shopping cart.

A guy stole my wife's car. I haven't reported it yet. Her mother was asleep in the back seat. I figure when she wakes up he will be glad to return it.


## Work – Employment

Work is good for you. I think I will save some for tomorrow

I'm not homeless, I just have chronic unemployment.

I'm not afraid of work. I could sit beside it and feel comfortable.

White collar workers should be sure and get a tan while on vacation. You don't want your boss to think you looking for another job.

We have a staggered lunch hour. Everyone drinks

I don't want to say he was getting desperate, but he saw a newspaper headline that said, "Man wanted for murder in Chicago" and he applied for the job.

They are brothers. One is in politics and the other one is honest.

He applied for a job at a motion picture studio. They wanted a man to die in a half empty saloon. He has been doing that for years.

He was a mind reader. He went to Hollywood and starved to death.

I was in the habit of getting $5,000 a week. This job cured me of that habit.

This is a non-profit organization. But we didn't plan it that way.


One: How many people actually work here?
Two: About half of them.



## Stephen Write Quotes
*One of the best deadpan one liner comedians. His jokes are funny, clean and his timing is impeccable.*


I used to work in a fire hydrant factory. You couldn't park anywhere near the place.


I stayed up all night playing poker with Tarot cards. I got a full house and 4 people died.


I went to a furniture store looking for a decaffeinated coffee table.


What is another word for "Thesaurus"?


Sometimes when I am bored, I like to go downtown and find a great parking place and sit in my car and count how many people ask me if I am leaving.

I bought some batteries, but they weren't included. So, I had to buy them again.


When I was a kid I had a quicksand box in my backyard. I was an only child. Eventually.


For my birthday I got a humidifier and a dehumidifier. I put them in the same room and watched them fight it out.

I got my driver's license photo taken out of focus on purpose. Now when I get pulled over the cop looks at it and says, "Here, you can go."

I went to a general store, but I couldn't buy anything specific.

I spilled spot remover on my dog. Now he's gone.

My neighbor has a circular driveway. He can't get out.

I bought some powdered water and I don't know what to add.

I put some instant coffee in a microwave oven and it went back in time.


I bought a house on a one-way dead-end street. I don't know how I got there.

I bought a house on a one-way dead-end street and now I can't get out.

I have a hobby. I collect sea shells. I keep them scattered on beaches all over the world. You may have seen some of them.

Hermits have no peer pressure.

When I think of my past, it brings up so many memories.

There's a fine line between fishing and just standing on the shore like an idiot.

How much deeper would the ocean be if there were no sponges?

It doesn't matter what the temperature is in the room, It is always room temperature.

Yesterday my eye glasses prescription ran out.

I was hitch-hiking the other day. A hearse pulled up and I said, "No thanks I'm not going that far.

I make my own water. Two glasses of "H" and one glass of "O".


## Jokes that do not fit in any category (I can think of)

Joke: I got up on the wrong side of the bed this morning. Normally that would not be a bad thing except my bed was on the third floor by an open window.

### The telephone rings.

"Hello, Senor Roy?  This is Ernesto, the caretaker at your country house in Mexico."

"Ernesto, It's 3 O'clock in the morning What is it?  Is there a problem?"

"Um, I am just calling to advise you, Senor Roy, that your parrot, he is dead".

"My parrot?  Dead?  The one that won the International competition?"

"Si, Senor, that's the one."

That's a pity! I spent a small fortune on that bird. Why is that so important to call me in the middle of the night? What did he die from?"

"From eating the rotten meat, Senor Roy."

"Rotten meat? Who fed him rotten meat?"

"Nobody, Senor. He ate the meat of the dead horse."

"Dead horse? What dead horse?"

"The thoroughbred, Senor Roy."

"My prize thoroughbred is dead?"

"Si, Senor Roy, he died from all that work pulling the water cart."

"Are you insane? What water cart?"

"The one we used to put out the fire, Senor."

"Fire? What fire are you talking about, man?"

"The one at your house, Senor! A candle fell, and the curtains caught fire."

"Was there much damage?"

"Si, the house she is all gone senor Roy."

"What? Are you saying that my 75-million-dollar mansion is destroyed because of a candle?!"

"Si, Senor Roy."

"The house has an electric generator what was the candle for?"

"For the funeral, Senor Roy."

"For the funeral. WHAT FUNERAL??!!"

"Your wife's funeral Senor Roy.

"My wife?"

Si. She showed up very late one night and I thought she was a thief, so I hit her with your new Ping G30 titanium head golf club with the TFC 149D graphite shaft."

SILENCE ........... "Ernesto."

"Si?"

"if you broke that driver, you're fired!"


Do twins ever realize that one of them is unplanned?

If poison expires is it more poisonous or is it no longer poisonous?

Which letter is silent in the word "Scent," the S or the C?

Why is the letter W, in English, called double U? Shouldn't it be called double V?

Maybe oxygen is slowly killing you and it just takes 75-100 years to fully work.

The word "swims" upside-down and backwards is still "swims".

Intentionally losing a game of rock, paper, and scissors is just as hard as trying to win.

100 years ago, everyone owned a horse and only the rich had cars. Today everyone has cars and only the rich own horses.

Your future self is watching you right now through memories.

If you replace "W" with "T" in "What, Where and When", you get the answer to each of them.

If you rip a hole in a net, there are actually fewer holes in it than there were before.

If 2/2/22 falls on a Tuesday, we'll just call it "2's Day". (It does fall on a Tuesday)

100 years ago, a Twenty Dollar bill and a Twenty Dollar gold piece were interchangeable. Either one would buy a new suit, new shoes and a night on the town. The Twenty Dollar gold piece will still do that.

## **Jewish tie salesman.**

A fleeing terrorist, desperate for water, was plodding through the Afghan desert when he saw something far off in the distance. Hoping to find water, he hurried toward the mirage, only to find a very frail little old Jewish man standing at a small makeshift display rack - selling ties.

The terrorist asked, "Do you have water?
The Jewish man replied, "I have no water. Would you like to buy a tie? They are only $5."

The terrorist shouted hysterically, "Idiot Infidel! I do not need such an over-priced western adornment- I spit on your ties. I need water!

"Sorry, I have none - just ties - pure silk – and only $5."

"Pahh! A curse on your ties, I should wrap one around your scrawny little neck and choke the life out of you, but I must conserve my energy and find water!"

"Okay," said the little old Jewish man, it does not matter that you do not want to buy a tie from me or that you hate me, threaten my life and call me infidel. I will show you that I am bigger than any of that. If you continue over that hill to the east for about two miles, you will find a restaurant. It has the finest food and all the ice-cold water you need...Go in Peace!

Cursing him again, the desperate terrorist staggered away over the hill.

Several hours later, he crawled back, almost dead and gasped, "They won't let me in without a tie!"

I was reading about the recession the other day. Did you know we were in a recession?  I realized we were in a recession when. . .

I got a pre-declined credit card in the mail.

On Wednesday my doctor takes off to play miniature golf.

A guy had an exorcism but couldn't afford to pay for it, and they re-possessed him!

A truckload of Americans was caught sneaking into Mexico.

Now a picture is only worth 200 words.

I have a step ladder. I never knew my real ladder.

My friend asked me to help him round up his 37 sheep. I said "**40**."

Just to show you how out of touch I am, up until this last week, I thought Roe vs. WADE was the decision Washington had to make. . . before he crossed the Delaware river.

What do you call a fish without an I? Fshhhhh. The hearer of this joke hears fish without an **eye.**

Fish sing out of tune because you can't tune a fish. (tuna fish)

In the 1400's a law was set forth in England that a man was allowed to beat his wife with a stick no thicker than his thumb.
Hence, we have 'the rule of thumb'

Q. What do bulletproof vests, fire escapes, windshield wipers and laser printers have in common?
A. All were invented by women.

In Shakespeare's time, mattresses were secured on bed frames by ropes. When you pulled on the ropes, the mattress tightened, making the bed firmer to sleep on. Hence the phrase...'Goodnight, sleep tight'

True story, or at least I think it is. The first couple to be shown in bed together on primetime TV was Fred and Wilma Flintstone

Well, that is all I got for this book. I hope you get plenty of laughs from these

Proof

Made in the USA
Columbia, SC
15 June 2018